rugger bugger blokes

Peter Slater

"Victory is the prize, Pain is the price"

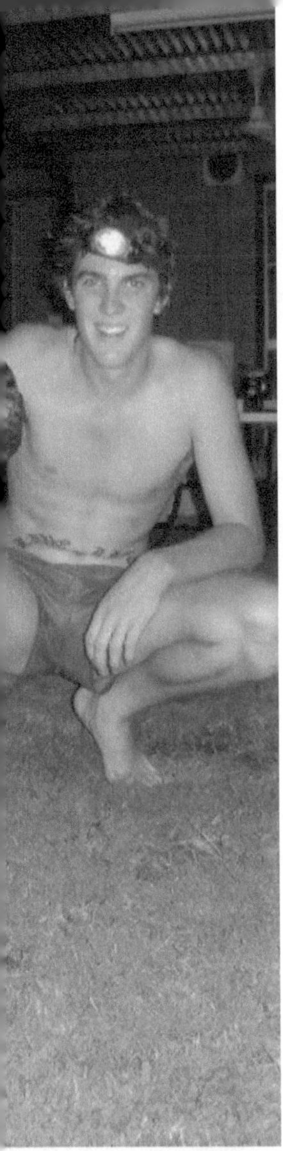

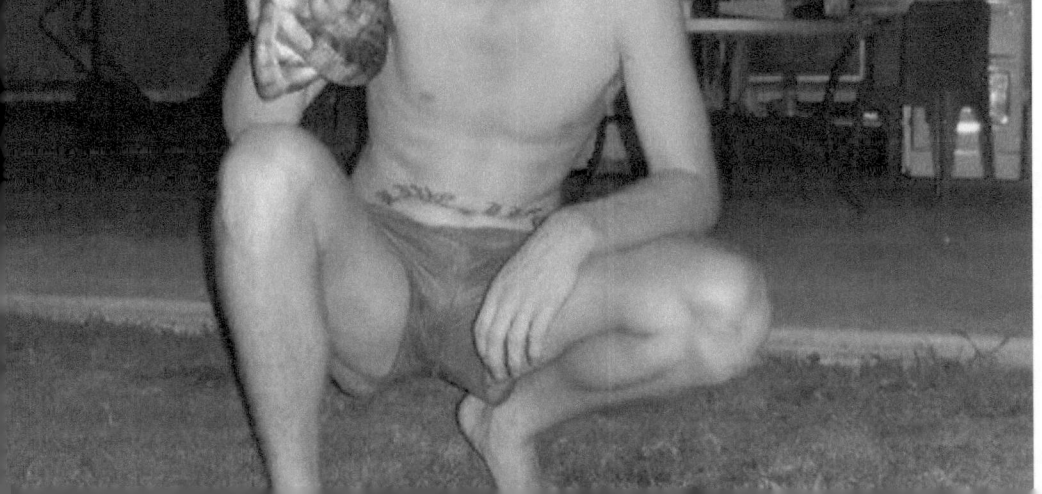

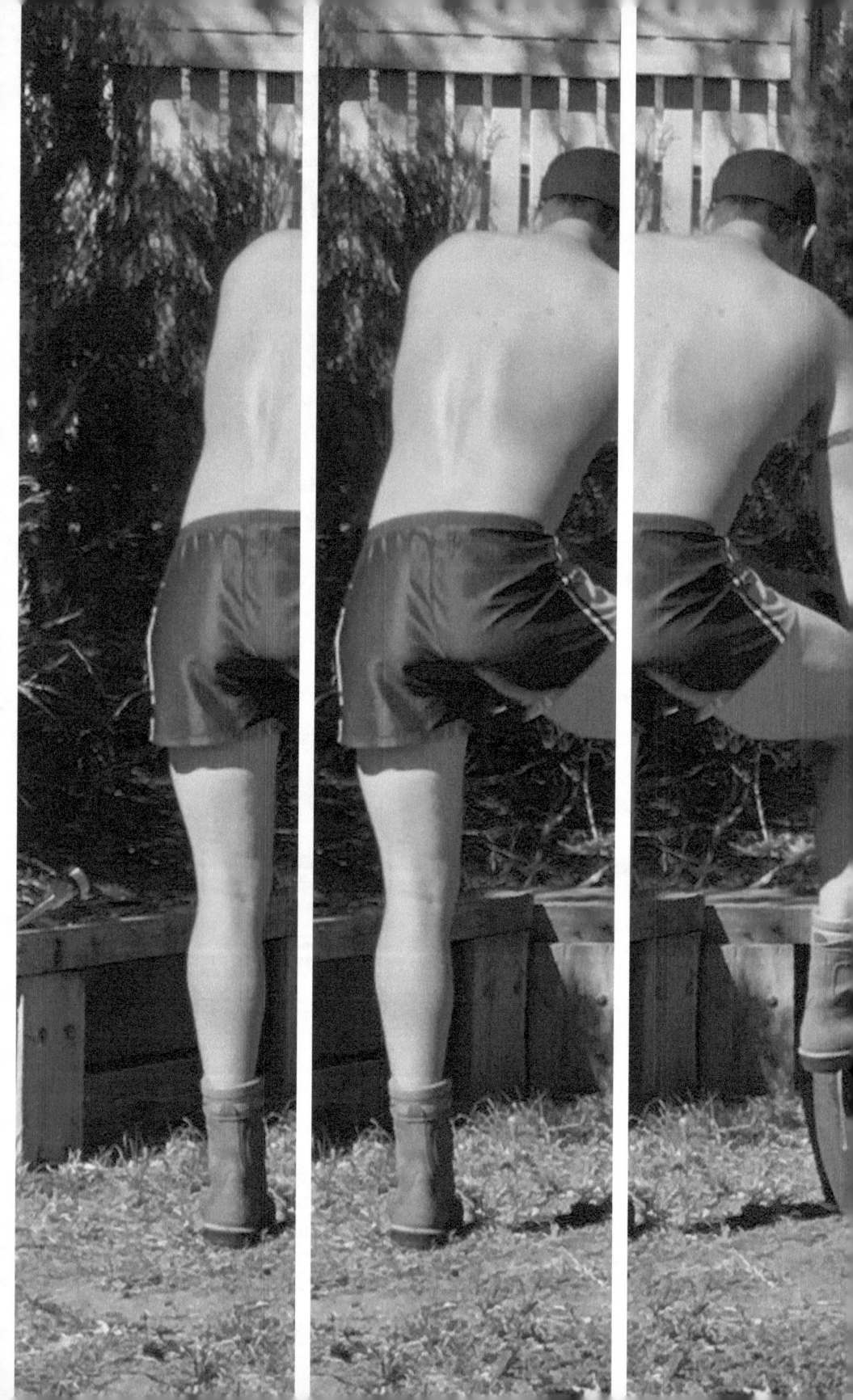

"PAIN IS YOUR FRIEND, IT REMINDS YOU, YOU ARE STILL ALIVE"

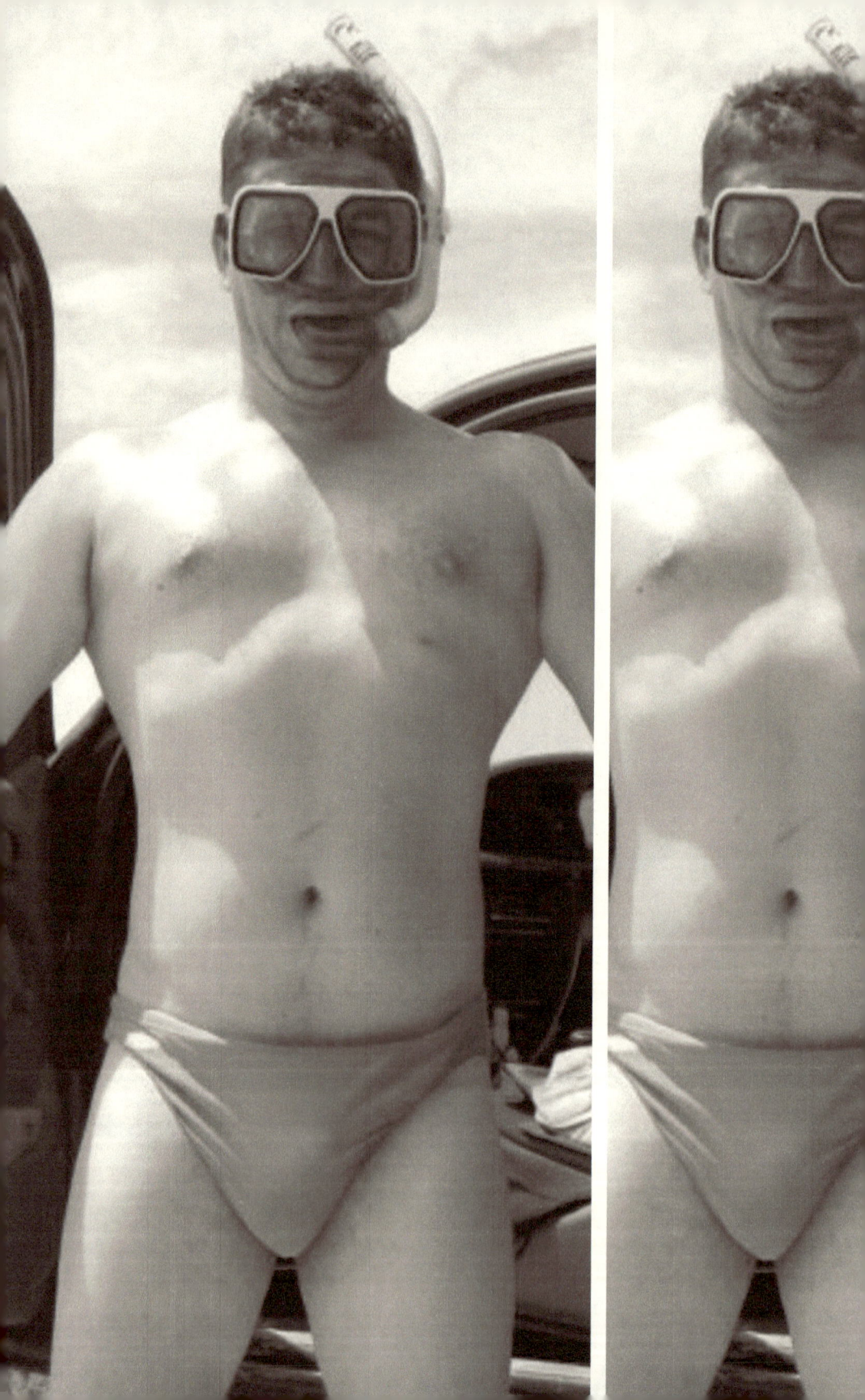

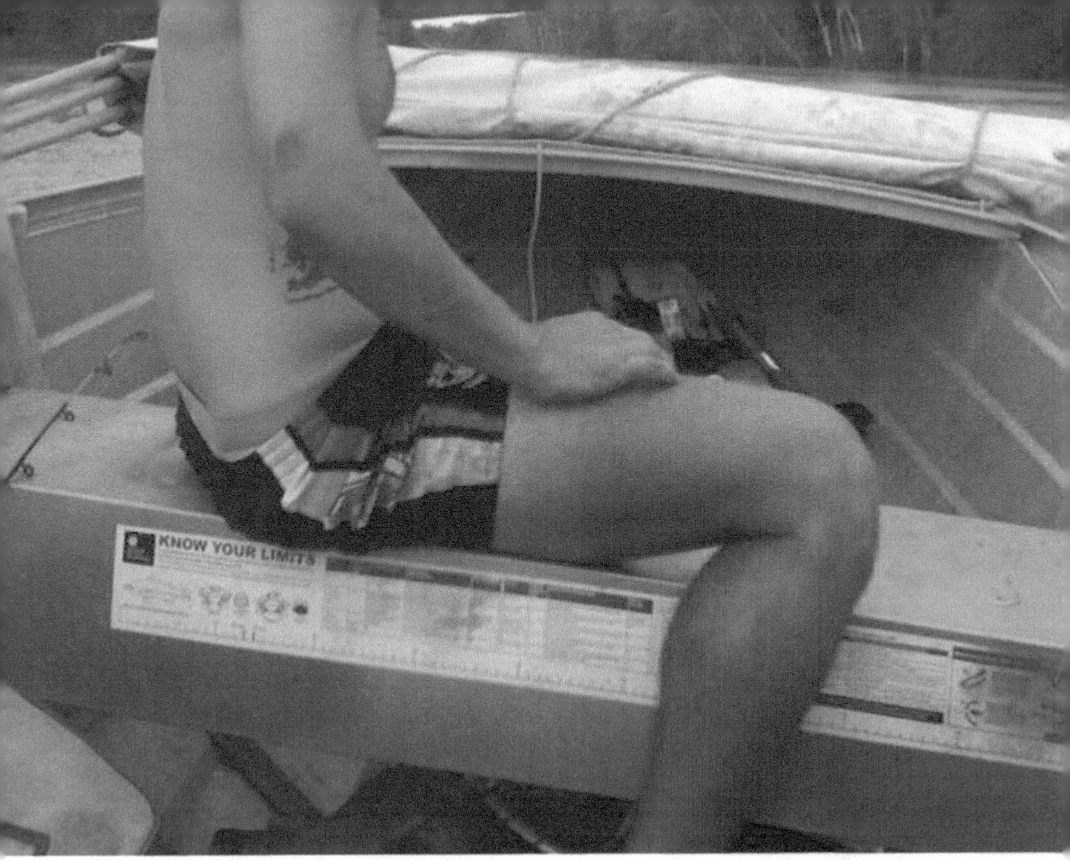
KNOW YOUR LIMITS

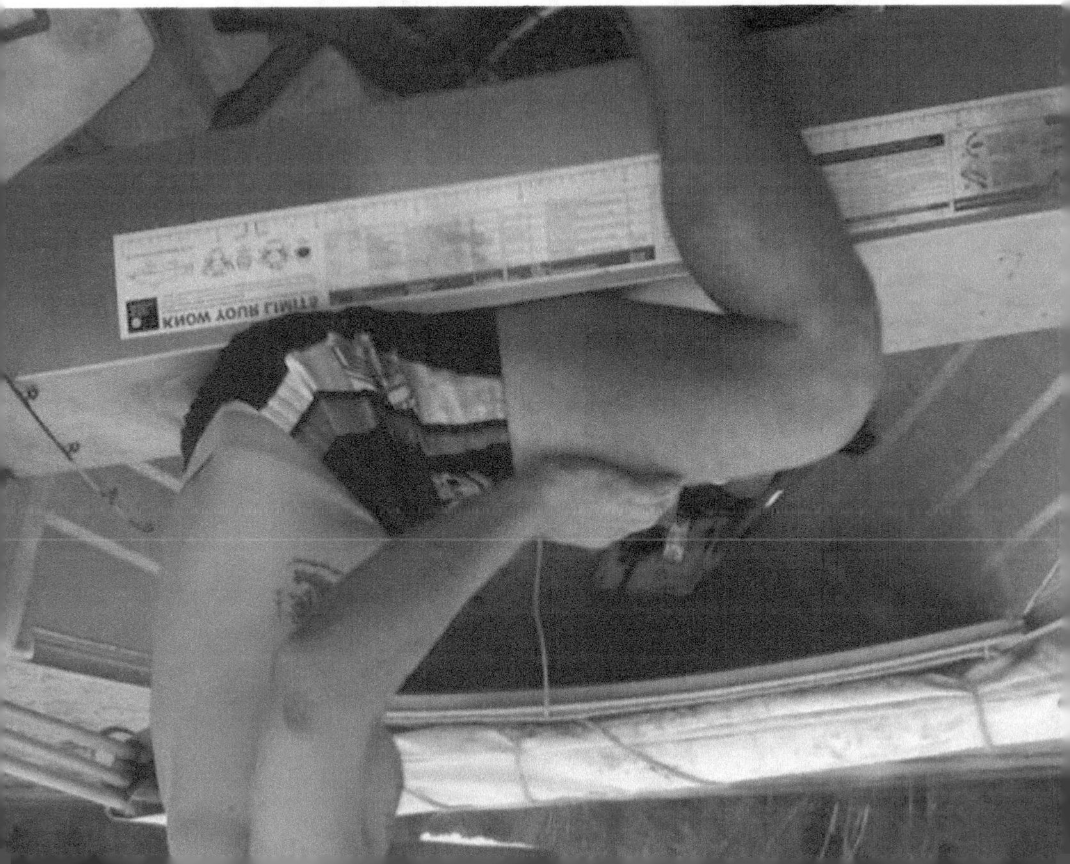

"RUGBY IS LIFE, THE REST ARE JUST DETAILS"

DOOKIE
THUNDER

DOOKIE
THUNDER

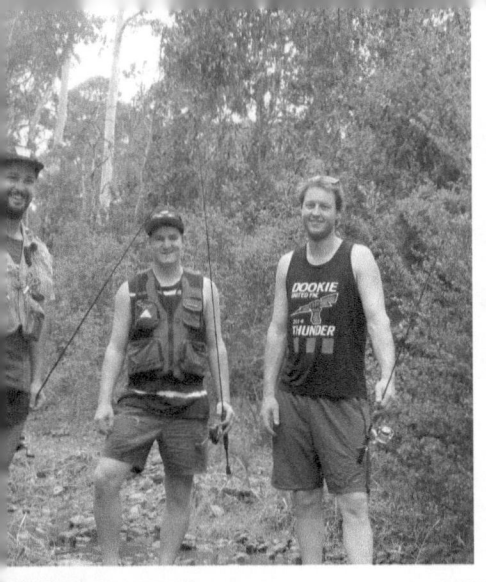

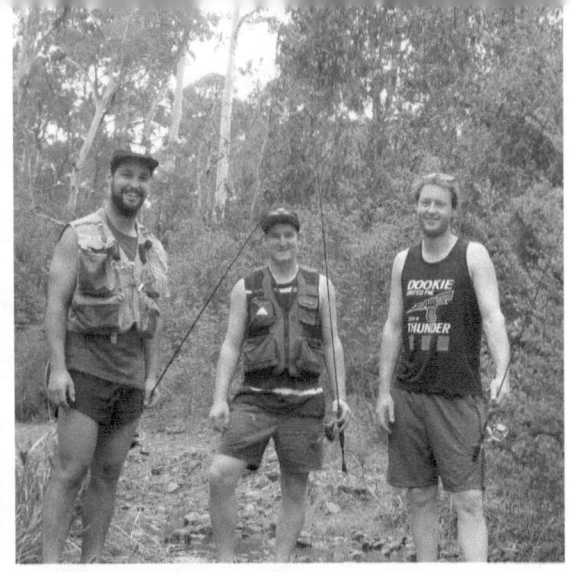

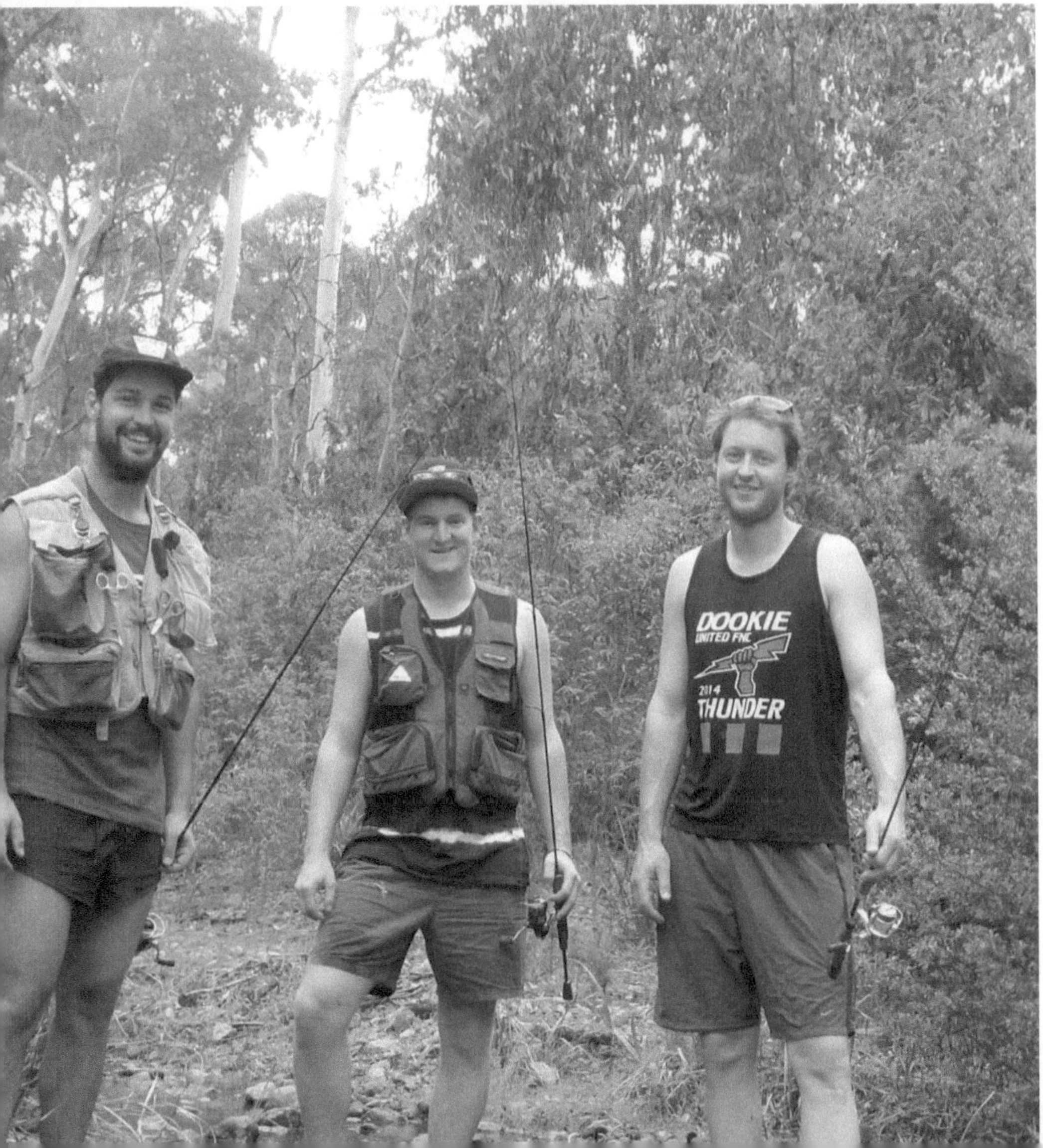
DOOKIE
UNITED FNC
2014
THUNDER

"RUGBY IS NOT JUST A SPORT, IT'S A WAY OF LIFE"

"TOGETHER EVERYONE ACHIEVES MORE"

"TRAIN AS YOU PLAY"

"WINNING ISN'T EVERYTHIN G. IT'S THE ONLY THING"

"RUGBY IS NOT A CONTACT SPORT, IT'S A COLLISION SPORT"

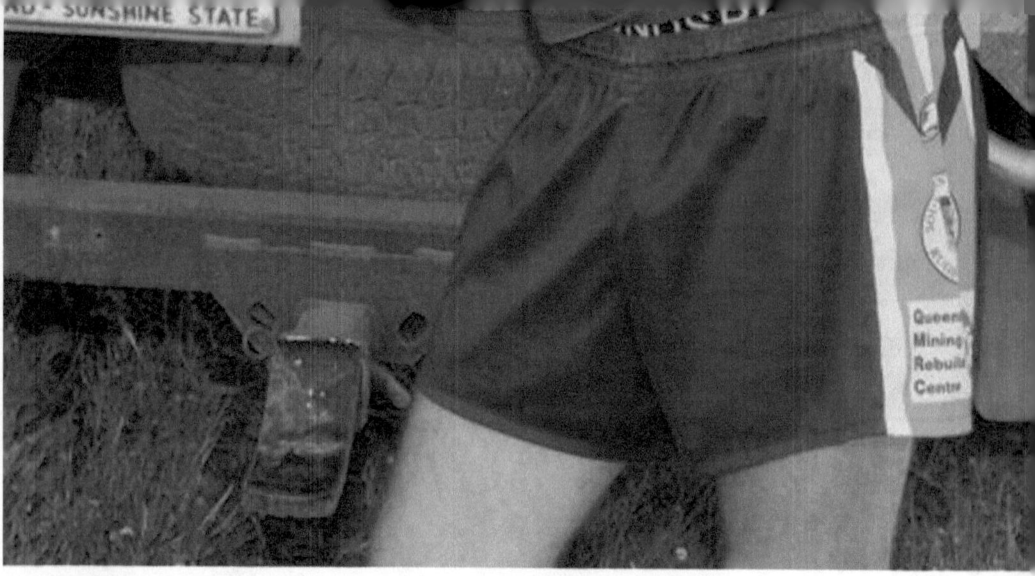
SUNSHINE STATE
Mining
Centre

BULLZYE
0·KKY
SUNSHINE STATE
Mining

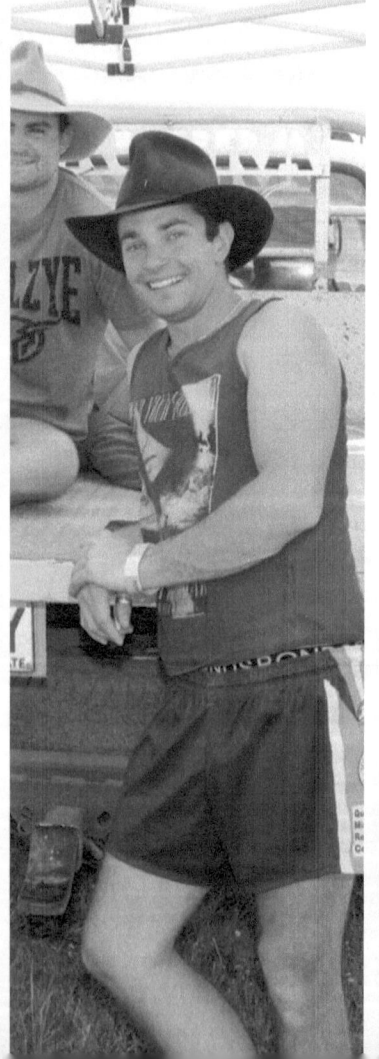

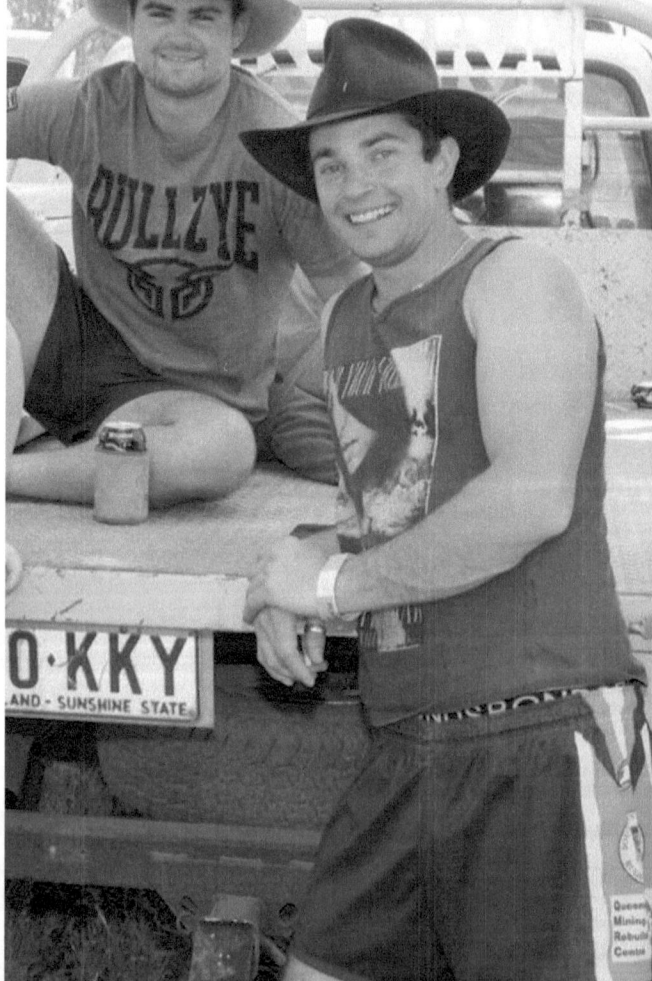

"TRAIN HARD, PLAY HARD, DRINK HARD"

"DONT
HATE THE
GAME, HATE
THE
OPPONENT
PLAYER"

HOT CHOOKS
FREE RANGE
EMU
HOT CHOOKS
FREE RANGE
EMU
HOT CHOOKS
FREE RANGE
EMU
HOT CHOOKS
FREE RANGE
EMU

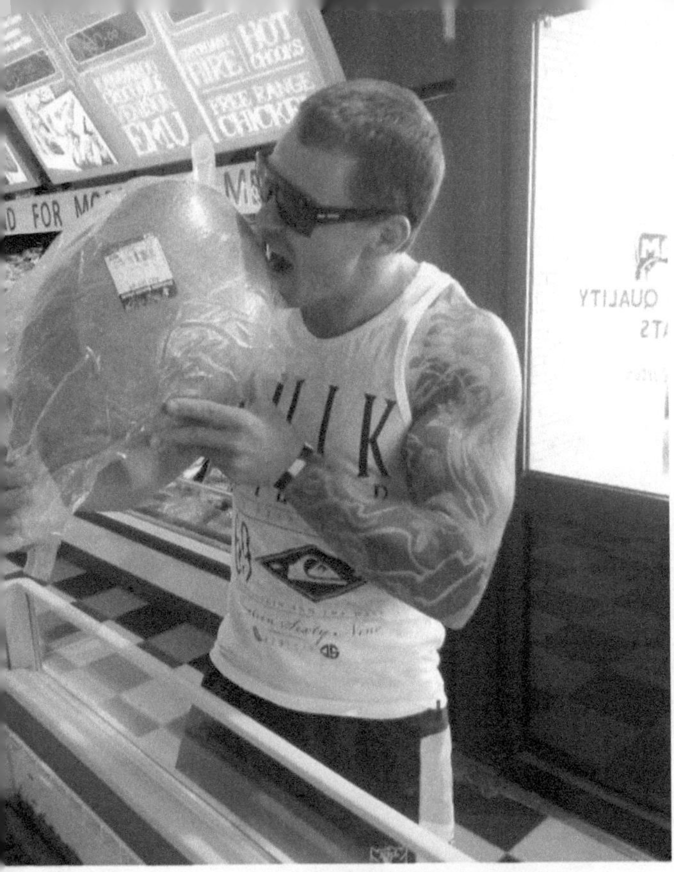

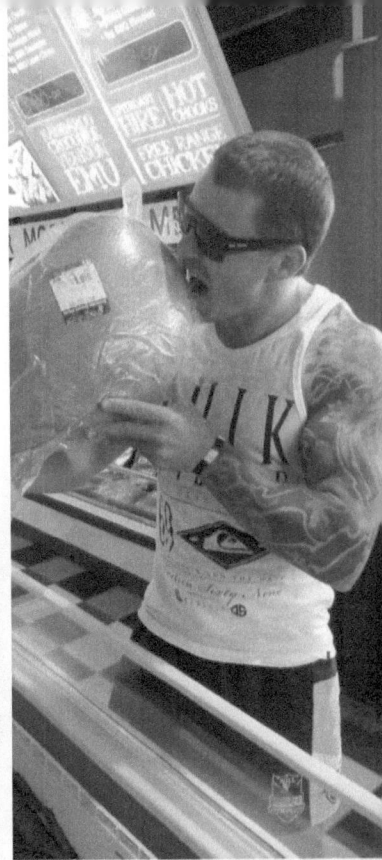

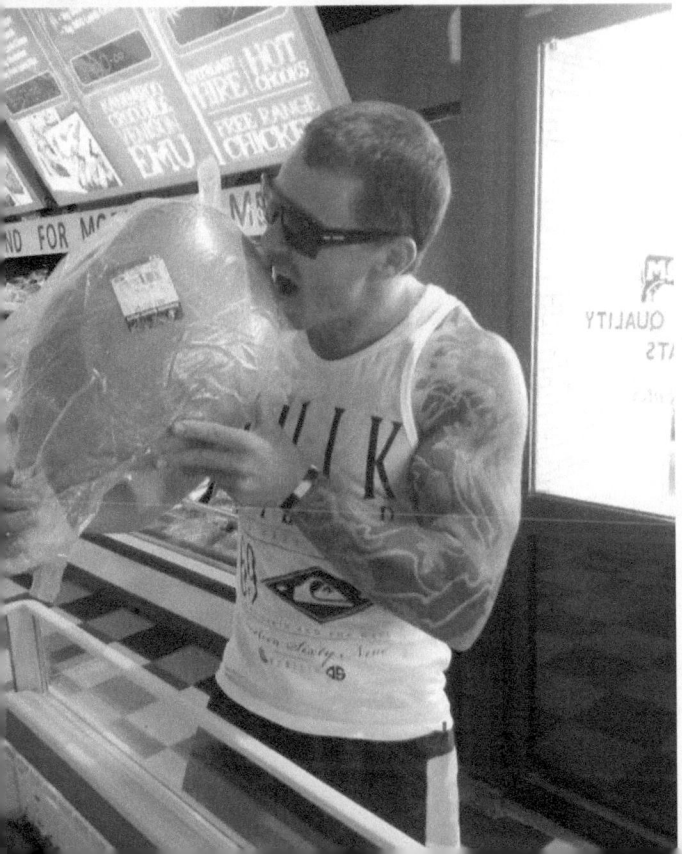

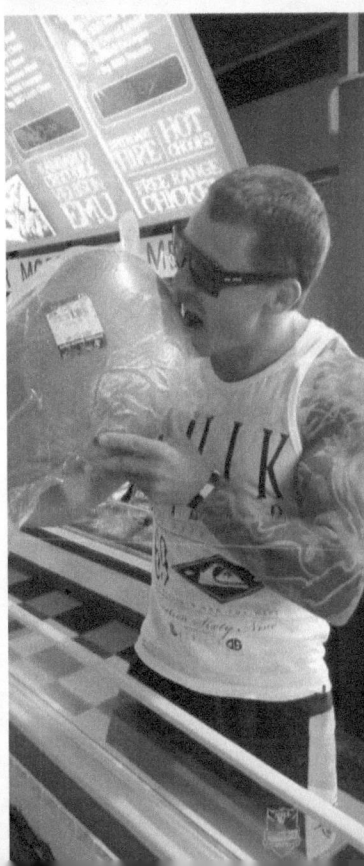

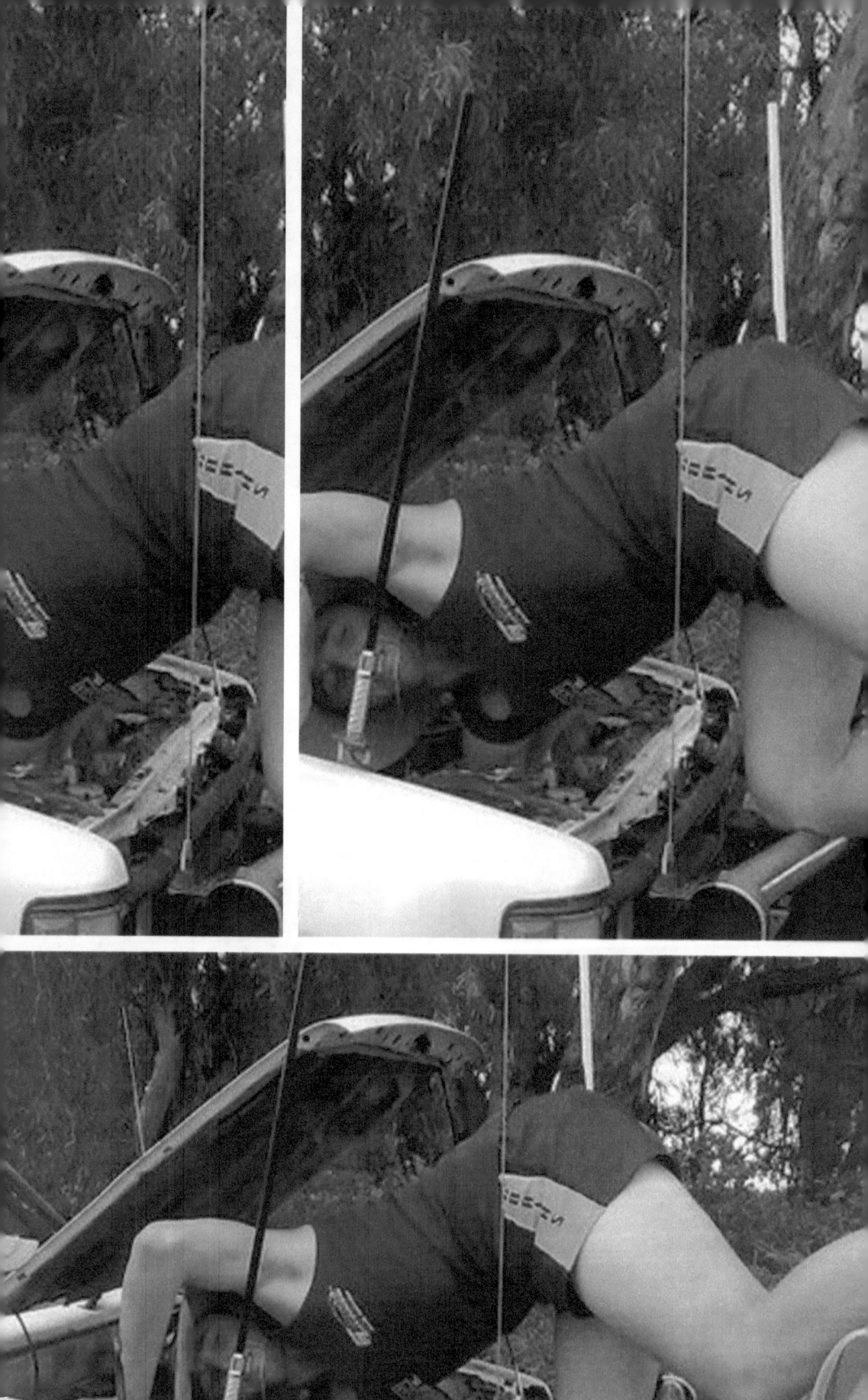

"FAILURE IS THE ROAD TO SUCCESS"

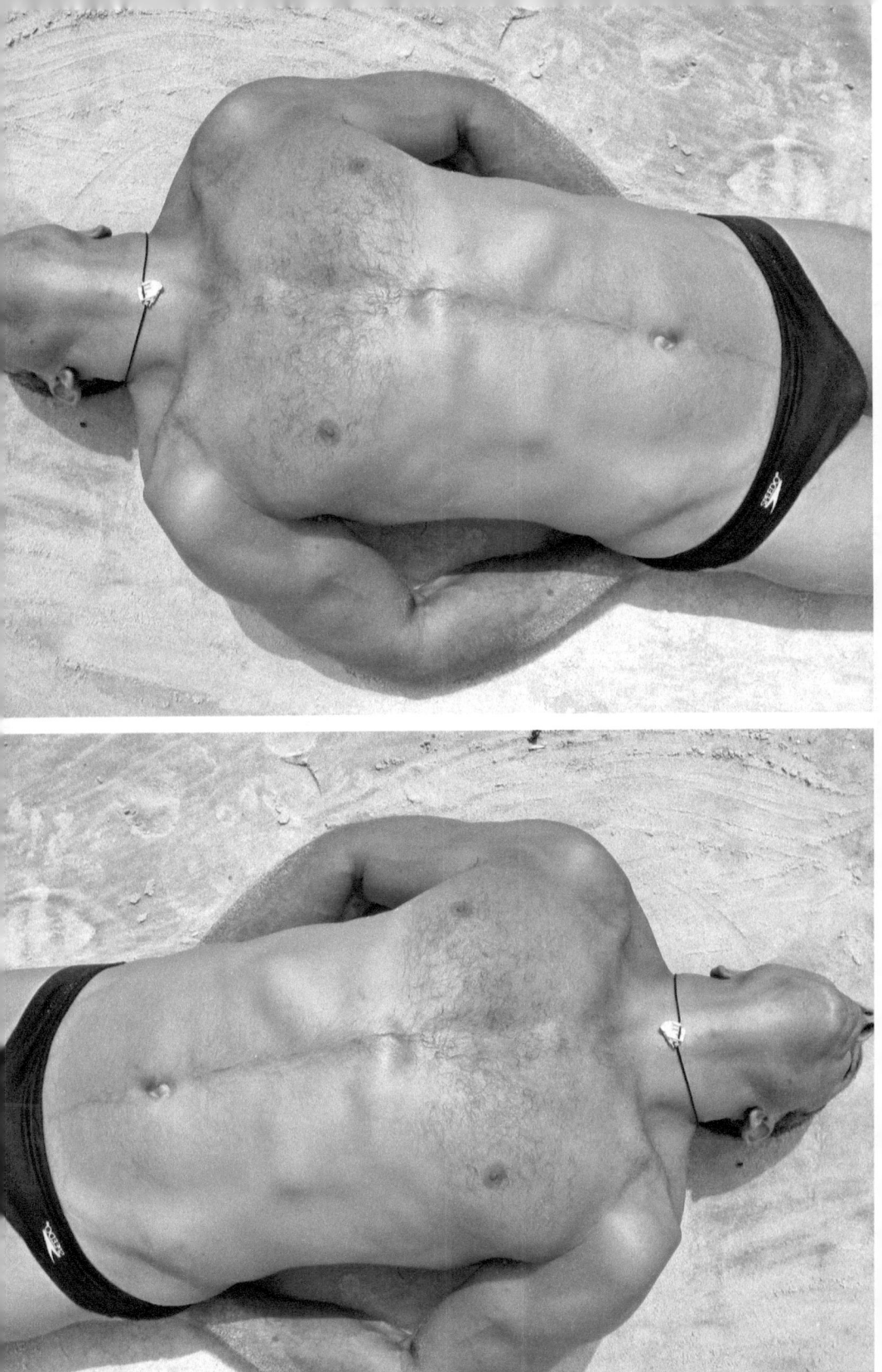

"THE ONLY PAIN IN RUGBY IS REGRET"

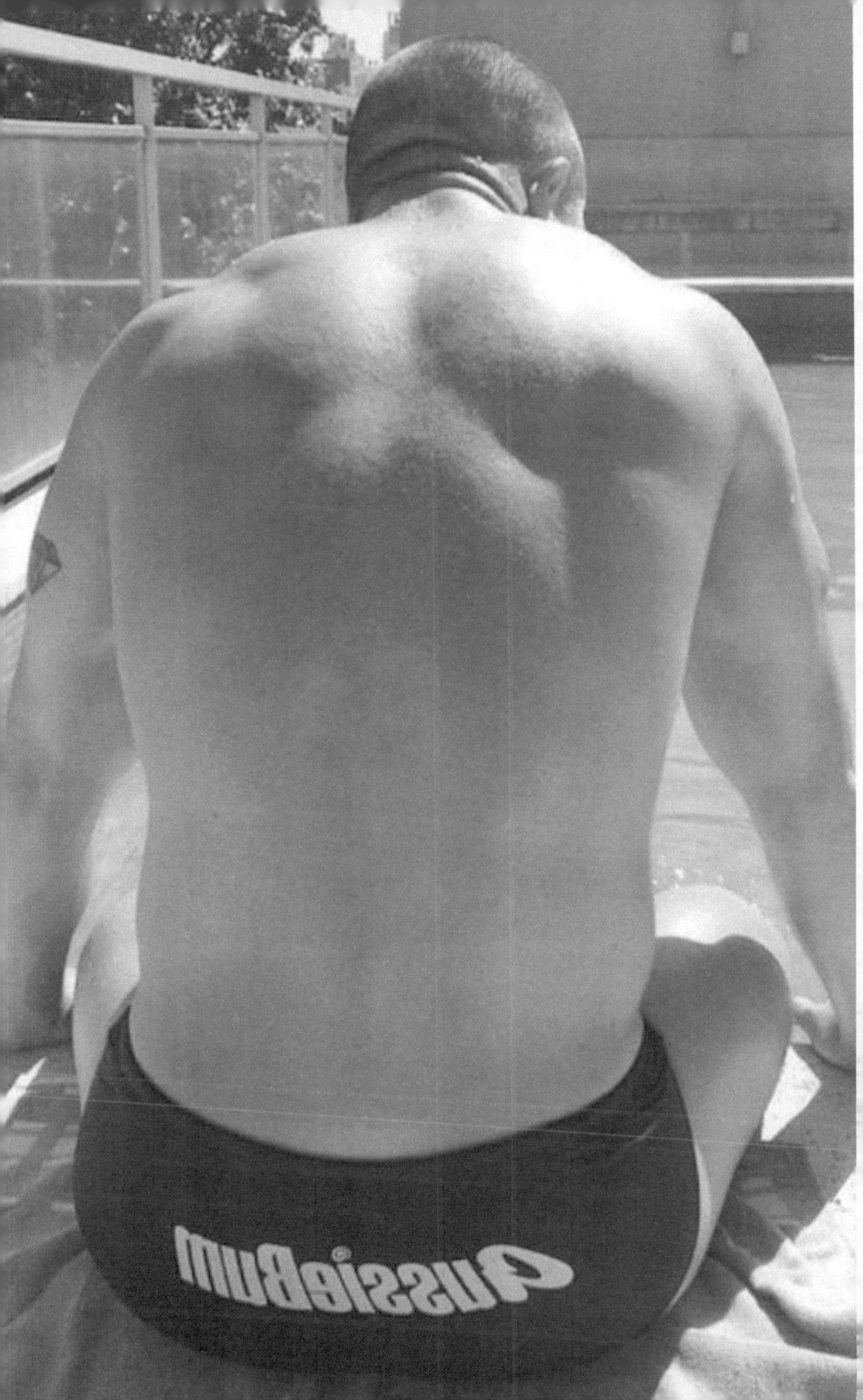

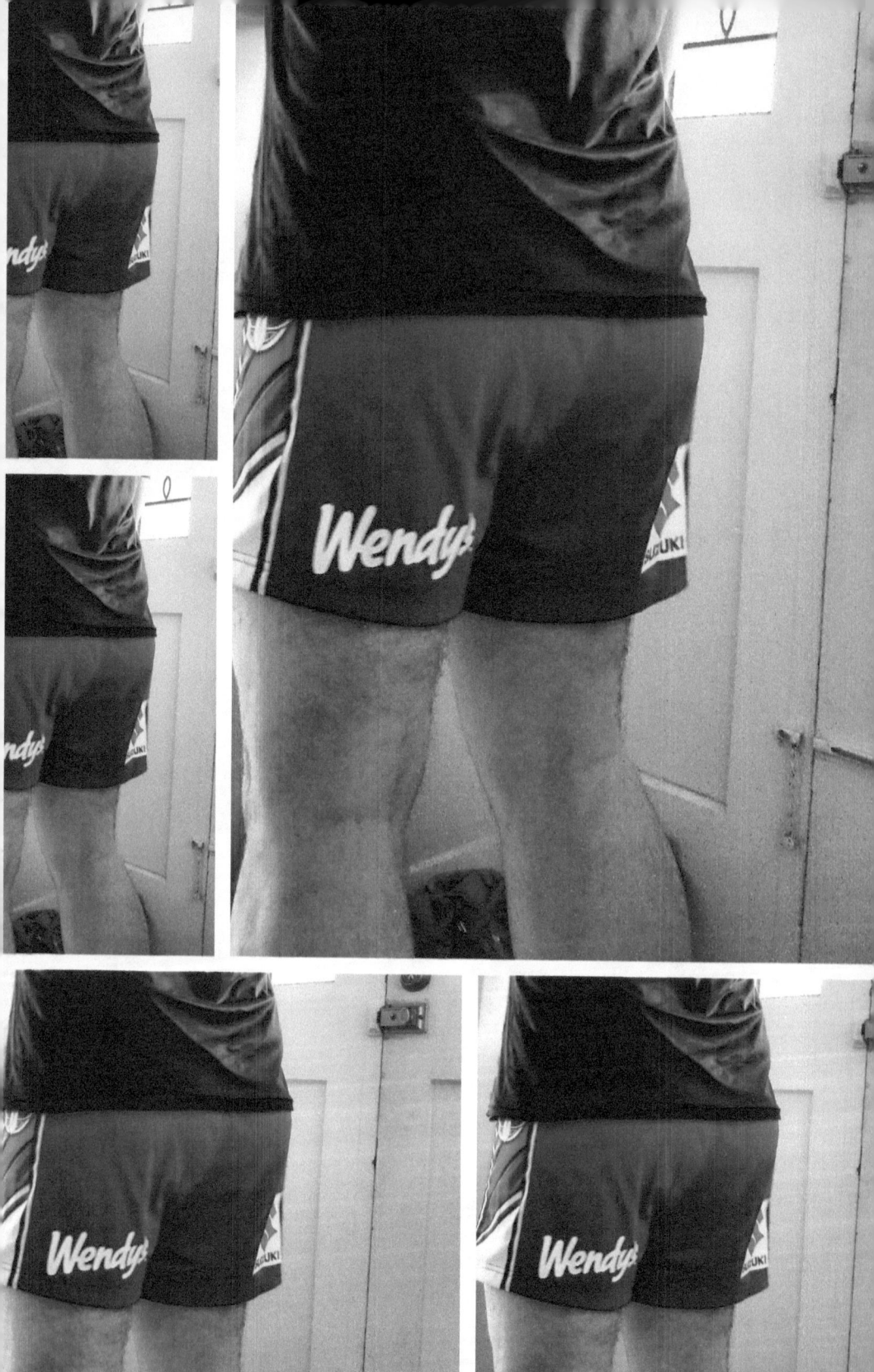

"WHEN YOU
MESS WITH
ONE
RUGGER,
YOU MESS
WITH THEM
ALL"

"NEVER TOO PRETTY TO PLAY RUGBY"

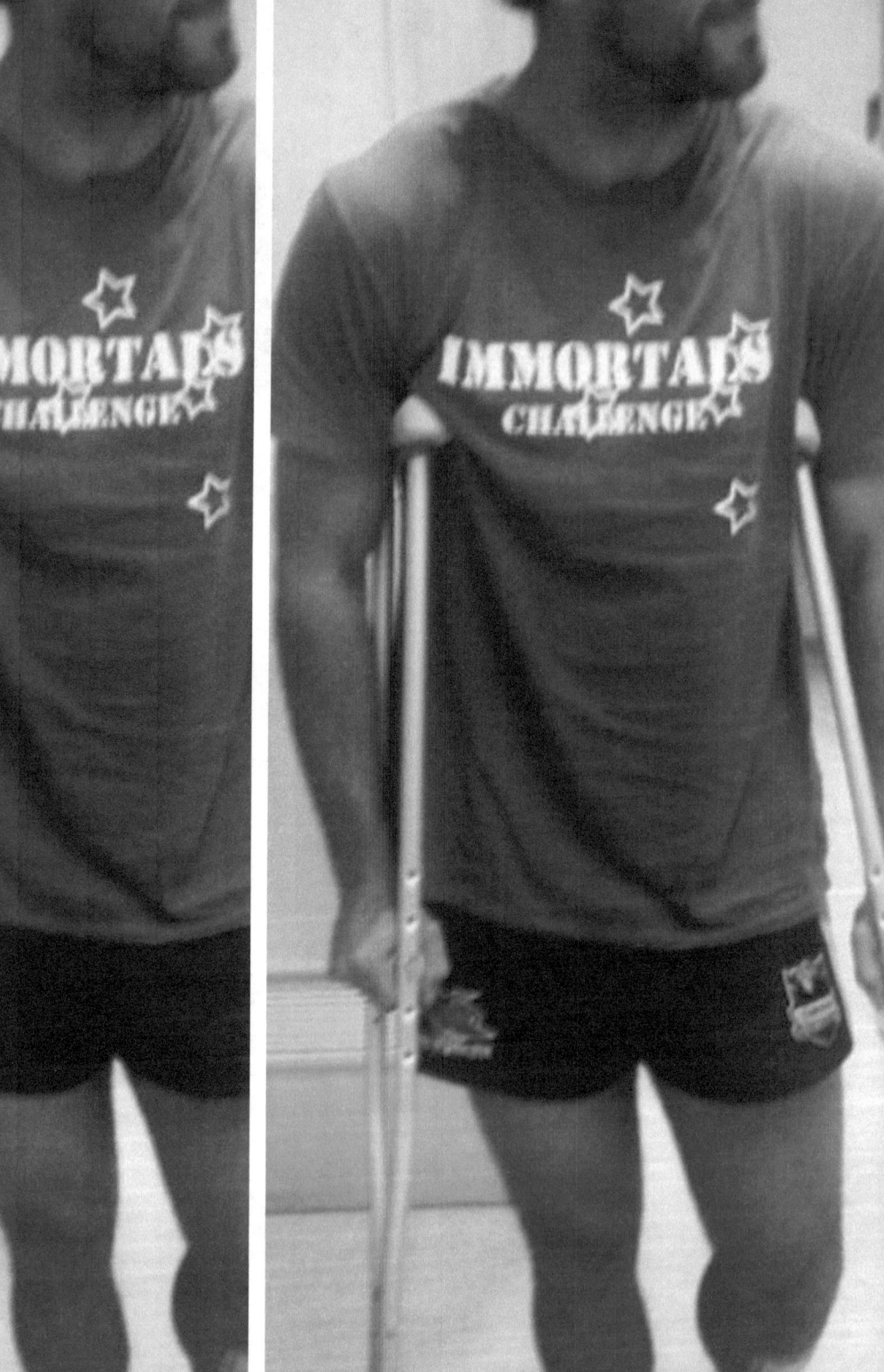

www.ingramcontent.com/pod-product-compliance
Lightning Source LLC
Chambersburg PA
CBHW021230280526
45784CB00005B/2037